FIRST LIGHT

FIRST LIGHT

poems by

David Wagoner

An Atlantic Monthly Press Book
Little, Brown and Company   Boston/Toronto

FIRST EDITION

Acknowledgments appear on pages 113–114.

Library of Congress Cataloging in Publication Data
Wagoner, David.
 First light.
 "An Atlantic Monthly Press book."
 I. Title.
PS3545.A345F5 1983   811'.54   83-12003
 ISBN 0-316-91708-7
 ISBN 0-316-91709-5 (pbk.)

ATLANTIC–LITTLE, BROWN BOOKS
ARE PUBLISHED BY
LITTLE, BROWN AND COMPANY
IN ASSOCIATION WITH
THE ATLANTIC MONTHLY PRESS

HP
Designed by Susan Windheim

*Published simultaneously in Canada
by Little, Brown & Company (Canada) Limited*

PRINTED IN THE UNITED STATES OF AMERICA

For Robin, for the first time,
with all my love,
and to the memory of my mother and father

CONTENTS

FIVE: *The Land behind the Wind*

SIX

ONE

THE TRUANT OFFICER'S HELPER

My only day in the black
Old truant officer's truck,
Grandfather and I
Went lurching and jouncing
Over raw country roads
To find boys playing hooky.
Their mothers on sagging porches
With steel-gray hair coming down
The sides of their sad faces
Would say they didn't know
What their boys were up to
Or where in the world they were,
But my grandfather knew.

His voice as calm and soft
And sure as during grace,
He told their mothers on them:
They were fishing in Sippo Creek
Or fighting in alleys
Or playing with guinea pigs
In back of the hospital
Or sniping butts in gutters
Or swimming and taking leaks
In the town's pure drinking water,
Not listening to their teachers,
Not learning their three Rs.

Bad boys stayed out of school
With no excuse from doctors

Or mothers, dentists or fathers.
We hunted them everywhere:
In orchards and vacant lots,
In carbarns and pool halls
And down by the canal
Where bums held their own classes,
All those tempting places
I might have gone myself
If I'd been old
Or bad or brave enough.

By afternoon we'd caught
Only one guilty sinner
Red-handed with swiped berries,
Red hair still wet,
A trespassing skinny-dipper
From out at the gravel pit,
And we brought him back alive
To Henry Wadsworth Longfellow
Junior High School, hanging
His head. Grandfather told him
Never to yield to temptation,
Never to steal or tell stories,
To grow up good and smart
As a Presbyterian,
Then sent him to his Doom.

My mother knew where *I* was
And gave me a good excuse:
I was helping my grandfather
Find bad boys and refill
The shelves of a magic storehouse,
A cave of Ali Baba,
With jars of paste and notebooks
And chalk and bottles of ink
And rubber stamps and rulers.
Longfellow over the door
Told us the thoughts of youth
Were long, long thoughts, but mine

In that dim supply room
Were short as my light fingers.

That night in a shed loft
I flew with a featherbed
By lamplight, writing my first
Short story full of lies
About a secret country
And a boy who disobeyed
And ran away in a dream.
I tried hard to be good
And smart and made it up
Out of my own head
On that stolen paper,
My stolen pencil trembling.

THE BAD UNCLE

The aunts couldn't stand to have Uncle Emmett doing
Anything he felt like oh he was into
Everything he was making so much noise
That Fourth of July it was impossible
To hear themselves think except out loud
With potash and sulfur paste between two bricks
Across the road by the cowshed swinging a spikemaul
Down to explode that horrible sandwich
Boom till cows and chickens wouldn't come home
To roost at milk-time the neighbors wandered in
To see what in thunder the big commotion oh
Emmett stop it he gobbled up half the pie
Before nephews and nieces got started for heaven
Sakes it was trouble enough him creeping around
To paint respectable barns with funny sayings
Like COWPIE PALACE YOUR BARNDOOR'S OPEN snoring

With his gypsy's face in church and his missing fingers
That scrawled comical notes on toilet paper oh
Emmett keep out keep away you'll sour the cream
The meringue won't stiffen and where where in the mercy
Did all those pickled eggs when everyone high
And low was looking for Emmett to find out why
When what he was doing so they could tell him
To quit so skinny he'd ought to be plumb
Tuckered by now like all the berry-picking
Good uncles pitching horseshoes or plucking mandolas
Off-key by the croquet court under green apples
By finally softening twilight oh for the land
Of the living what's Emmett up to with David crouching
Behind two telephone poles with what in the world
Two skyrockets in the dusk no roman candles oh
Emmett teaching David to shoot out sputtery sparkly
Streaky red after white after dangerous tremendous blue look
Fireballs at each other in his best corduroy
Duelling a black hole burnt in his shirt oh my
Aunt Dorothy wide as a doorway letting him be
Independent pregnant again with love
The only one smiling not clucking or bellowing
Or shying away out of pure exasperation
Among the homegrown buttery flock of others oh
Emmett the bad example was a caution.

THE SHOCKING MACHINE

It looked like something stolen
Out of a horror movie:
The brass hardware, the flanged
Knobby and hinged braces
Rescrewed to mahogany
From the handy-dandy cadaver

Of our old player-piano
All varnished like a coffin
Except for two steel handles
Beside an induction coil
From the corpse of our Chrysler.

The god in the machine
Was an eight-volt battery,
And the god sparkling behind it
My inventive eccentric mad
Boy scientist of a father.
He wanted to be my teacher,
To be greater than the real one
Who'd done Ben Franklin's trick
With a kite and key and lightning.
He wanted to be somebody
Remarkable, wanted me
To love him and didn't know
How else to show me how
Except by turning us loose
With this shocking contraption
In the neighborhood to lose
Our friends and influence people.

Oh boy, the big idea
Was to find the dumb ones
Daring enough to hang
On hard, and then you pushed
The switch and rang their doorbells!
We watched their arms go stiff
At the elbows! Their hair stood up!
Their spines shook all the way
From their skulls to their butt bones!
And their mouths flew open
To let out yelps or screams!
Or sometimes, for whole
Wonderful split-seconds
In a row, nothing
But air! And we'd go ape

And cackle, crow, and guffaw
At this fantastic fun
His father had taught *him*.
We doubled up! We roared
Like fiends at the jerkiness
Of others, at awkwardness,
Embarrassment, and pain,
The bad parts we kept hidden
Deep in our own dungeons.

But our peasants caught on fast.
In no time, they'd all learned
The worst about us two
Shakers, shockers, and makers
Of comic turns and twitches
All flesh and crazybones
Are the crazily resurrected
And disinherited heirs to:
They hadn't just been stuck
With the sons of Frankensteins
But with two sad monsters.

THE BEST SLOW DANCER

Under the sagging clotheslines of crepe paper
By the second string of teachers and wallflowers
In the school gym across the key through the glitter
Of mirrored light three-second rule forever
Suspended you danced with her the best slow dancer
Who stood on tiptoe who almost wasn't there
In your arms like music she knew just how to answer
The question mark of your spine your hand in hers
The other touching that place between her shoulders
Trembling your countless feet light-footed sure

To move as they wished wherever you might stagger
Without her she turned in time she knew where you were
In time she turned her body into yours
As you moved from thigh to secrets to breast yet never
Where you would be for all time never closer
Than your cheek against her temple her ear just under
Your lips that tried all evening long to tell her
You weren't the worst one not the boy whose mother
Had taught him to count to murmur over and over
One slide two slide three slide now no longer
The one in the hallway after class the scuffler
The double clubfoot gawker the mouth breather
With the wrong haircut who would never kiss her
But see her dancing off with someone or other
Older more clever smoother dreamier
Not waving a sister somebody else's partner
Lover while you went floating home through the air
To lie down lighter than air in a moonlit shimmer
Alone to whisper yourself to sleep remember.

AFTER THE HIGH-SCHOOL GRADUATION, 1944

Who was I over the top
Rung of the ladder leading
Nowhere but up up
Into the night declaiming
Out of the wonder
Of original whiskey
My first glass first class first
Prize speech to the ranks
Of houses emptied
Of their sons in the dark is life
So dear or peace so sweet oh

Patrick Henry rousing
My carousing classmates
Ghostly below me leaping
The sawhorse staggering
Through zigzag rails
To crawl to the swinging bars
And the mudpit galloping
Together they thought now
Forever over the playground
Rebuilt for the building
Of our bodies' marvelous war
With each other as we were
What we were starlit performers
Reconquering all
Obstacles where what it was
That gentlemen wished
What they would have
For graduation was the gift
Of my voice making the most
Of treason by exercising
The clash of resounding arms
Around legs and bodies no longer
School spirited away
By teachers but by a primed
Loaded good cheerleading
Petty class officer
Me with the last word
On the subject of the unknown
Sheepskinned soldiers not death
That night but liberty.

MY FATHER IN THE BASEMENT

Something had gone wrong down in the basement.
Something important needed rearranging
Or shaping up down there like the neat shadows
He kept in the coal bin and under the workbench.
But when he went to find it, he couldn't find it.

None of the fuses had blown as dark as storms
At their tiny portholes. Nothing was on fire
But the fire in the furnace, and nothing was frozen
But the humming freezer and the concrete floor
And the hands he'd poured it with, now cold and hard.

Had his mother sent him there to fetch crab apples,
Spicy and gold, or piccalilli for supper?
Was that his father shouting and then turning
A deaf ear to his answer? It was cold
And hard to remember why he wasn't working.

So he lay down on the floor, doing things right
The first time because nothing was worth doing
Unless he did it himself. There was no use
In calling strangers if something was out of order
Because if he couldn't fix it, nobody could.

ELEGY FOR MY MOTHER

She heard the least footfall, the least sigh
Or whisper beyond a door, the turning
Of a page in a far room, the most distant birdsong,

Even a slight wind when it was barely
Beginning: she would wait at a window
For someone to come home, for someone sleeping

To stir and waken, for someone far away
To tell her anything she could murmur
Word for word for years, for those close by

To be alive and well in stories she loved
To listen to all day, where life after life
Kept happening to others, but not to her,

And it was no surprise to forget herself
One morning, to misplace wherever she was,
Whoever she was, and become a ghostly wonder

Who would never wonder why it didn't matter
If no one listened to her or whether
She was here or there or even somewhere

Or why it felt so easy not to linger
In the doorway saying hello, goodbye, or remember
Me, but simply to turn and disappear.

THEIR BODIES

to the students of anatomy at Indiana University

That gaunt old man came first, his hair as white
As your scoured tables. Maybe you'll recollect him
By the scars of steel-mill burns on the backs of his hands,
On the nape of his neck, on his arms and sinewy legs,
And her by the enduring innocence
Of her face, as open to all of you in death
As it would have been in life: she would memorize
Your names and ages and pastimes and hometowns
If she could, but she can't now, so remember her.

They believed in doctors, listened to their advice,
And followed it faithfully. You should treat them
One last time as they would have treated you.
They had been kind to others all their lives
And believed in being useful. Remember somewhere
Their son is trying hard to believe you'll learn
As much as possible from them, as *he* did,
And will do your best to learn politely and truly.

They gave away the gift of those useful bodies
Against his wish. (They had their own ways
Of doing everything, always.) If you're not certain
Which ones are theirs, be gentle to everybody.

TWO

FEEDING

When I dropped bread, they swam
Out of nowhere, the fingerling
Catfish, even darker
Than the pool lying dead calm
Over them and around them.

Those inches of black ribbon
All held white crumbs like eyes
And wavered themselves away
In schools and disappeared
Again into deeper water.

When I dropped more, what came
Was an altogether stranger
Nature of moving slow,
As though the elders knew
They could be slow to swim

But would still be in time
To take what was their own
Into their own gloom
Of soft-barbed opening
And closing jaws and turn

Away in easy curves
With a sinewy suppleness,
Undulant, fading down
To what they might become
Somewhere still more dim.

When I broke the final crust,
What rose to the underface

Of the pond (so slow, it seemed
Too slow to lift a form
That huge from so far under)

Has kept its place in the night
Of my mind since I was four,
Moving its perfectly sure,
Unhurried, widening mouth
Toward whiteness to darken it.

THE OTHER HOUSE

As a boy, I haunted an abandoned house
Whose basement was always full of dark-green water
Or dark-green ice in winter,
Where frogs came back to life and sang each spring.

On broken concrete under the skeleton
Of a roof, inside ribbed walls, I listened alone
Where the basement stairs went down
Under the water, down into their music.

During storms, our proper house would be flooded too.
The water would spout from drains, through the foundation
And climb the basement stairs
But silently, and would go away silently,

As silent as my mother and father were
All day and during dinner and after
And after the radio
With hardly a murmur all the way into sleep.

All winter, the frogs had slept in an icy bed,
Remembering how to sing when it melted.

If I made a sound, they stopped
And listened to me sing nothing, singing nothing.

But gradually, finally April would come pouring
Out of their green throats in a green chorus
To a chorus me home toward silence.
Theirs was the only house that sang all night.

IN THE PLAZA DE TOROS

Madrid, September 1956

Six bulls. And three young men,
Three novilleros, had come
To kill them, to earn
At their first corrida (and mine)
The name of matador.

The parade of the bright cuadrillas,
Picadores on old geldings,
The brandishing of cornets,
And a bull came rushing through
Death's Door, looking like death,
Enormously black, outraged
By what this scene might be,
Quivering, quick, horns high.

While *pics* with their Don Quixote
Lances lowered those horns
By piercing, muscle-wrenching,
Fat-and-lean punishment
In spite of the bone-breaking
Lunges against live horsehide,
The first novice stared
Hard from the barrier

In his unscarred suit of lights
Like an aristocrat
Insulted by a peasant.
He entered, flourished his cape,
Was hooked, tossed twice, and killed.

It happened just like that.
And after the stunned *chulos*
Had carried his body off
At a run, the next in order
Came out, out of tradition,
To fight before his turn,
To finish that incompleteness.

He was as tall and handsome
As the Dawn of a New Regime,
And he smiled grimly, gamely
Above backsliding feet
Till, trembling, sword in hand,
He was gored high in the groin,
Spun up and around and down.
It took him days to die.

The third, a slim dark frowning
Round-shouldered hollow-eyed
Hesitant solemn gypsy,
Faced all six bulls alone.
He finally killed the killer
But clumsily and "badly,"
And the Plaza whistled him
To scorn and cheered the bull.
But more and more skillfully,
"Bravely" and bravely,
He dealt with the others.

Four more times his sword
Between huge shoulder-bones
Plunged deep into a lung,
And the mule team trotted on

To drag black shapes away
To the place where the meat goes.
After five, his face went gray
Under the falling flowers,
And the sixth was nearly the dance
Aficionados pray for
In honor of darkness.

The President gave him an ear
(For a novice, almost Glory),
And while the band thrust home
Ear-piercing *pasodobles*,
He toured the bloody sand
High on his world's shoulders.

Had any other tourist
Out in the sun-swept bleachers
Or the nearer, more costly shadows
Been as full of Dominguín
And Hemingway as *I'd* been?
Did anyone leave as empty?
I could hardly tell the gardens
Of Spain from the Guardia Civil
Or death in the afternoon.

If the gypsy isn't dead
By now, does he feel, as I do,
That something of his died
Back then (whatever he did
In the long meanwhile
Or earned or learned to want)
And was hauled away in chains
By mules or by strange hands
To be honored under the knives
Of doctors or pious butchers
For the gaping mouths of the poor? —
That he lost that day, forever,
Some unforgivable hunger?

THE AUTHOR OF *AMERICAN ORNITHOLOGY* SKETCHES A BIRD, NOW EXTINCT

(Alexander Wilson, Wilmington, N.C., 1809)

When he walked through town, the wing-shot bird he'd hidden
Inside his coat began to cry like a baby,
High and plaintive and loud as the calls he'd heard
While hunting it in the woods, and goodwives stared
And scurried indoors to guard their own from harm.

And the innkeeper and the goodmen in the tavern
Asked him whether his child was sick, then laughed,
Slapped knees, and laughed as he unswaddled his prize,
His pride and burden: an ivory-billed woodpecker
As big as a crow, still wailing and squealing.

Upstairs, when he let it go in his workroom,
It fell silent at last. He told at dinner
How devoted masters of birds drawn from the life
Must gather their flocks around them with a rifle
And make them live forever inside books.

Later, he found his bedspread covered with plaster
And the bird clinging beside a hole in the wall
Clear through to already-splintered weatherboards
And the sky beyond. While he tied one of its legs
To a table-leg, it started wailing again

And went on wailing as if toward cypress groves
While the artist drew and tinted on fine vellum

Its red cockade, gray claws, and sepia eyes
From which a white wedge flowed to the lame wing
Like light flying and ended there in blackness.

He drew and studied for days, eating and dreaming
Fitfully through the dancing and loud drumming
Of an ivory bill that refused pecans and beetles,
Chestnuts and sweet-sour fruit of magnolias,
Riddling his table, slashing his fingers, wailing.

He watched it die, he said, with great regret.

A REMARKABLE EXHIBITION

*Its diving ability in dodging at the flash of a gun
is well known. I once saw a remarkable exhibition
of this power by a loon which was surrounded by gunners
in a small cove on the Taunton River.*

— Arthur Cleveland Bent, *Life Histories
of North American Diving Birds*, 1919

It was remarkable, that day on the river
When eight gentlemen hunters in tweeds and gaiters,
Some firmly on shore and some wading through rushes,
Put a loon to the test.
A light mist hovered in shreds, but for all intents
It was a commonplace morning, sunlit and windless,
Affording a clear view of the clear water
And its reflective surface.
Their rifles were bench-sighted, their aim steady,
And though they varied as marksmen from indifferent
To expert, when the loon appeared out of nowhere
Beside them suddenly

At such close range, it seemed impossible
A bird of its size could dodge so many bullets
From unforeseeable angles more than a moment.
Across that cove
The sound of their guns went crackling and echoing
Under the pines, reechoing and colliding
Like the eccentric ripples that broke reflections
Around the loon's white breast
And starry back. It lifted its dark neck
And darker head and beak to go arching under,
And every time it plunged, they thought it was dying,
But it would rise
Again whole minutes later unnaturally
Far off, unexpectedly, in unpredictable
Directions, breathe, swivel and arch to dive
Again, and be gone.
They were genuinely amazed at a performance
That round for round matched theirs. It lasted longer
Than any of them could agree on through that winter
Over their hearthstones
When they recounted the tale and their cartridges
And tried to guess the mechanics of its defense
Aside from stubbornness and web-footed power
And those amber eyes
They couldn't help recollecting: how could they be
Magic enough to avoid eight rifles flashing
As long as all that and still, as they finally were,
Be closed in death?

TO A FARMER WHO HUNG
FIVE HAWKS ON HIS BARBED WIRE

They saw you behind your muzzle much more clearly
Than you saw them as you fired at the sky.
You meant almost nothing. Their eyes were turning
To more important creatures hiding
In the grass or pecking and strutting in the open.
The hawks didn't share your nearsighted anger
But soared for the sake of their more ancient hunger
And died for it, to become the emblem
Of your estate, your bloody coat-of-arms.

If fox and raccoon keep out, your chickens may spend
Fat lives at peace before they lose
Their appetites, later on, to satisfy yours.
You've had strange appetites now and then,
Haven't you. Funny quickenings of the heart,
Impulses not quite mentionable
To the wife or yourself. Even some odd dreams.
Remember that scary one about flying?
You woke and thanked the dawn you were heavy again.

Tonight, I aim this dream straight at your skull
While you nestle it against soft feathers:
You hover over the earth, its judge and master,
Alert, alive, alone in the wind
With your terrible mercy. Your breastbone shatters
Suddenly, and you fall, flapping,
Your claws clutching at nothing crookedly

End over end, and thump to the ground.
You lie there, waiting, dying little by little.

You rise and go on dying a little longer,
No longer your heavy self in the morning
But light, still lighter long into the evening
And long into the night and falling
Again little by little across the weather,
Ruffled by sunlight, frozen and thawed
And rained away, falling against the grass
Little by little, lightly and softly,
More quietly than the breath of a deer mouse.

FOR A FISHERMAN WHO
DYNAMITED A CORMORANT ROOKERY

Lean at your rail. Look close at the ripe water.
You've lived on it and off it, but now
Slip over and settle
Down in that world where your gill net or purse seine
Or trolling lures have been going *for* you.
Neck stretched, eyes open,
Your lubber's feet both paddling as well as they can
At a slant, deeper and deeper, your arms
Held stiff at your sides,
Your nose thrust to a point, do your best to follow
The wake of a better fisherman
Than you, the flight
Of the sleek swift cormorant plunging under the sea
At his labors, his weavings, his sudden
Changes of course beyond you
As he darts and lunges, then rises to the sun
With the rest of his short life
Quicksilver while he lifts

His slim blue-throated neck and his catch to the sky.
But stay where you are. Sink farther. Enjoy
The depths of rapture
Like other divers and sailors cast adrift
Under these waves. You've been here
Before, remember:
The salt of the earth and the old salt of the ocean —
On both sides of your skin they whisper
And turn to each other.
Though you act like a stranger, you have nothing to fear
From the fish around you. Like birds of passage
They're yours alone
Just as you thought. They're finally all yours.
They'll help you to balance that good nature,
To give your share
Of the wealth to mother-of-pearl and living spirals,
To put stars gently in your place,
To change your mind
By a sea change through which everything is forgiven,
Not given up for lost, not even
You disappearing.

THE HORSEMEN

All day we followed the tracks of the wild horses
On foot, taking turns at resting,
Eating our cold food as we walked each way
They turned to escape us. They disappeared
Sometimes behind rough-shouldered ridges, up canyons,
But we hurried after them and found them
Too soon for grazing. They swam rivers
That might have made them safe from wolves
But not from *our* hunger: it was behind our eyes
And not in our mouths. As we came nearer, nearer,

Their heads would turn to us, then turn
Away, they would go away aimlessly,
Hating our smell as we loved theirs and hating
The sight of us as we loved theirs, the headstrong
Round-rumped tangle-maned light-footed
Windy-tailed horses who would belong to us.

Already, others of our slow kind were flying
Above four hooves, their feet leaving the earth
Like birds flying as far in this new day
As five sleeps in the old. Now following after
At evening, we gave them no rest, gave nothing
But hunger and that other emptiness:
Fear of our strangeness. Some of us slept by water
While they stood in the distance, darkening,
Smelling it with dry nostrils, waiting to drink
As deep as the coming night but seeing us waiting
There for something they must have known was their hearts
And their whole lives to come.

In the morning, they were kneeling, lying down, rising
And trotting again, then slowing, walking no faster
Than we kept walking after them. They stumbled
And fell once more and stayed where they were
As if dying, their white-flecked mouths
And white-cornered eyes all turning
As we touched them on their trembling withers to tell them
What they were, what they would learn from us.

ELEPHANT RIDE

Under her heavy shoulder, the bulging cliffside
Of her haunch, the children are gazing up at her
(The trunk comes groping backwards, almost touching
Each of them) as they climb the ramp and clamber
High over sawdust onto a new life,
The glittering howdah, short legs straddling the gray
Wide world of her back now heaving them forward
And swaying under them all the way around
The ring through flash and spotlight and flashy brass
And the spin of guy-wires and balloons, loudspeakers
Blaring and faces over elephant ears
Only a moment forever there they were
Now being told to climb back down to the ground
Still underfoot, still there under their feet
To be walked on shakily together looking back.

THE ESCAPE FROM MONKEY ISLAND

For years they had looked at trees. They would sit all day
On stones, surrounded by water, and watch trees.
Then a branch in a storm at night came crackling
Down to bridge their moat, and they crossed over
And climbed those trees and waited for daylight.

In chorus then, they lifted wild new voices,
New sobs and cackles and hoots, new chatters

And screams and squeals of naked joy in the morning.
They moved past cages and walls through the highest limbs
High over the heads of keepers who called them
To come back tamely to that other kingdom.

But the day kept turning and branching. There were no islands
But branches like streams to follow, where they could cling
And sway, spread-eagling, stretching against the sky
Like prehensile stars, while keepers held up pears
And apples as red and yellow as caught sunlight.

By evening, hungry, all of them had fallen
Quiet, and they came slowly down to the ground
To be taken in, to spend their days on stones
For the mumbling and shuffling watchers, the upright ones
Who would stand under the trees, not dreaming of climbing,
Not dreaming of waking with the gift of tongues.

OCTOPUS

In her small yard of seabed and salt water
Whatever shape she finds (the coral
Or seaweed, both rust-red
As she is, or sand or cockleshells or the glass
Upright between us) she becomes.
Her languishingly easy
Arms become those shapes, the double rows
Of suckers fondling them, resolving
Other selves, no roughness
Or smoothness or ungainliness alien
To any of her changeable
Eight by infinite
Shiftings, not one surface or emptiness
Unknown, unfilled, or unfulfilled,

While floating above her
Under the tough soft pulsing hood of her mantle,
Her brain is fanning her gills, is closing
Her beaklike mandibles
To rasp her tongues on pieces of sea bass slowly,
Is slowly curling her arms, is staring
Steadily through round eyes,
Is lifting all thought of her to its beginning
Lightly, buoyantly, ready to leave
A darkness in its place.

PEACOCK DISPLAY

He approaches her, trailing his whole fortune,
Perfectly cocksure, and suddenly spreads
The huge fan of his tail for her amazement.

Each turquoise and purple, black-horned, walleyed quill
Comes quivering forward, an amphitheatric shell
For his most fortunate audience: her alone.

He plumes himself. He shakes his brassily gold
Wings and rump in a dance, lifting his claws
Stiff-legged under the great bulge of his breast.

And she strolls calmly away, pecking and pausing,
Not watching him, astonished to discover
All these seeds spread just for her in the dirt.

WASHING A YOUNG RHINOCEROS

Inside its horse-high, bull-strong, hog-tight fence
It will stand beside you in a concrete garden,
Leaning your way
All thousand pounds of its half-grown body
To meet the water pouring out of your hose
The temperature of September.

And as slowly its patina (a gray compounded
Of peanut shells and marshmallows, straw and mud)
Begins to vanish
From the solid rib-cage and the underbelly
Under your scrub brush, you see, wrinkled and creased
As if in thought, its skin

From long upperlip to fly-whisk gleam in the sun,
Erect ears turning backwards to learn how
You hum your pleasure,
And eyelashes above the jawbone hinges
Fluttering wetly as it waits transfixed
(The folds at the four leg-pits

Glistening pink now) for you never to finish
What feels more wonderful than opening
And closing its empty mouth
Around lettuce and grapes and fresh bouquets of carrots
And cabbage leaves, what feels as good to desire
As its fabulous horn.

WINTER WREN

It knows each leaf, it darts
Under each leaf so swiftly
It seems here there
Not there now clinging one
Instant to a frond, its quick
Brief thumb of a body gone
With a tail-flick among moss
And under the green roots
Of a stump in rain as soft
As moss and back again
Where suddenly it holds still
At the loud warning call
Of a thrush, long minute
After minute, motionless,
Becoming no wren now
But streaks of buff and umber
Beyond it, the stiff stems
And star-claws of dead leaves,
Disappearing no matter how
Hard my eyes may stare
At where it quickened,
Then faded to nothing
On earth as plain as daylight.

KINGFISHER

The blunt big slate-blue dashing cockaded head
Cocked and the tapering thick of the bill
Sidelong for a black eye staring down
From the elm branch over the pool now poised
Exactly for this immediate moment diving
In a single wingflap wingfold plunging
Slapwash not quite all the way under
The swirling water and upward instantly
In a swerving spiral back to the good branch
With a fingerling catfish before the ripples
Have reached me sitting nearby to follow it
With a flip of a shake from crestfeathers to white
Bibchoker down the crawhatch suddenly
Seeing me and swooping away cackling
From the belt streaked rusty over the full belly.

GOLDEN RETRIEVER

Dew-soaked and bleary-eyed with the smells of the field,
He zigzags out of cheatgrass and wild roses
And fallen thistles, as gold, as ragged, his tongue
Lolling, nose high, his breath trailing a mist
Over the empty weed-crowns as he drinks in
The whole morning at once, around his neck
A broken chain that follows him over hummocks
By sunlight on the sheen of cobwebs binding
The dead spikelets of grass and their living stems
And down through sedge and rushes along the creek
And up among brambles and arches of blackberry
To disappear in the light-filled field again.

LOONS MATING

Their necks and their dark heads lifted into a dawn
Blurred smooth by mist, the loons
Beside each other are swimming slowly
In charmed circles, their bodies stretched under water
Through ripples quivering and sweeping apart
The gray sky now held close by the lake's mercurial threshold
Whose face and underface they share
In wheeling and diving tandem, rising together
To swell their breasts like swans, to go breasting forward
With beaks turned down and in, near shore,
Out of sight behind a windbreak of birch and alder,
And now the haunted uprisen wailing call,
And again, and now the beautiful sane laughter.

*T*HREE

UNDER THE RAVEN'S NEST

On a branch still bobbing and weaving under the weight
Of his arrival, the raven begins squawking
With all the neck-stretched
Emphasis he can give to his great outrage.

He wants to know what I'm doing skulking so near
The Tree of Trees where he and his loud mate
Heaped up their nest last spring one scrap at a time
Thirty yards overhead and raised two fledglings.

They spent the living summer teaching their young
By diving like stooping hawks to frighten them
Through ecstasies of sideslips and wingovers
In the wind till both had memorized ravenhood.

He takes my measure with one eye, letting me have it:
Saw-whetting, chuckling, clock-winding, metallic gurgling,
Cackles and nutcracks, dogbarks and whistles,
Quick sotto voce lipsmacks, coos, and retchings.

Then leaving me with an impossible act
To follow, an *ars poetica* far beyond
Mere minor tricksters, he swerves to the cedar crown
And presides with lofty silence over my workroom.

THE STORYTELLER

We had no warning. He was suddenly there
Among us: an old man bent under the weight
Of the wind and years, his cloak in tatters, his face
Wrinkled and scarred, the chart of a wilderness.

He asked for nothing but began telling a story
Of a journey to a land where the moon burns
And the sun is a stone, where water stands or flows
In the place of air, where the air runs into pools

Or under the ground, where the ground is a whirl of stars
And the sky bursts green in spring and gold in winter,
Where through the trees grown down from heavy clouds
The fish come flying and singing from dusk till dawn,

Where slowly the silent birds swim through the earth
Like broken rainbows, where weather from storm to calm,
From frost to fire is born, not in the mountains
Or the sea, but behind the eyes of travellers.

Our sons and daughters, already clever liars
Themselves, knew he was lying, but they listened
All evening by firelight. At the story's end
He left no silence. He stood and began singing,

His voice from far away like the sound of the nameless
In a distant country praising their dead heroes,

Lamenting, but promising rescue for the dead.
Still singing, the old man walked into the night.

And one by one our children followed him
Without begging leave, without begging our pardon
And never returned except as voices in dreams
Warning us, softly troubling our troubled sleep.

MEDUSA'S LOVER

Her personal problems seemed unbearably
Embarrassing to Medusa: she hadn't a thing
To wear in public, and classical drapery
Did nothing to hide the hard-core facts of her figure,
And even the warmest, frilliest underclothes
Left her underworld colder. Her dreadful sisters,
Instead of comforting her in her misery,
Proved being a Gorgon ran in the family,
And she couldn't do a thing with her snaky hair
But feed it eggs and mice so it wouldn't, at night,
Hiss her awake or slither into her ears,
And worst of all, men couldn't catch her eye
Without turning as stony-faced as statues.

But suddenly one day to her amazement
She saw a young man shuffling toward her sideways,
Holding a shield like a mirror. He was staring
At her reflection, and though he wasn't too gorgeous
Himself — shoes down at the winged heels
And matted with mud, his roomy helmet wobbling
Around his head, the hem of his cloak sagging —
He was vastly more appealing than mere high-fliers,

Invincible soldiers, or invisible heroes:
He was looking at her and wasn't petrified.

She opened her arms to him. She lurched to meet him.
Her hair was hissing (in chorus) a wild love song.
She saw the gift he'd brought her: a gleaming, slender,
Adamantine sickle to wear like a queen's pendant
At her throat forever. She lifted her chin. She pursed.
She closed her eyes to wait for her first kiss.

PANDORA'S DREAM

Falling asleep, she saw the lid of the box
Beside her glittering, the unknown dowry
She was forbidden to look at,
But under eyelids heavier than moonlight
She carried that glitter down into a dream.

She was in the dark, in a chamber, touching its walls
And floor and ceiling with pieces of herself,
Some glinting like fireflies, some burnt black and cold,
Odd flapping and squirming pieces, feathered
And furred, bone-pointed, clawed, all wanting out.

But there was nowhere to go, no door, no window.
She was trapped as if in a box. Then with a groan
Of hinges, the ceiling opened,
And there in the widening strip of light, grown huge
And terrible, her own face looked in.

And all those parts of her in a swarm went flying
Upward and outward: maggots with bat wings,
Pink termites, scarlet bees, green wasps in a fury

And moths on fire like twistings of paper
And through them a death-squeaking of black mice.

She became that other holding the lid upraised
And wishing what she'd scattered would return
And shut itself in again to be forgotten,
That the god who'd cursed her with this gift
Would relent and rescue her from a curious heart.

She woke, she stretched, she forgot, she yawned, she saw
Only a box at her bedside, shimmering
With promises she could keep or break by lifting
A single clasp and using her naked eyes.
She rose, still in a dream, and opened it.

SLEEPING BEAUTY

The hard part wasn't the overgrown, thorn-clawed hedge
Between the Prince and what was supposed to be
A Beauty destined for him: rose-vines gave way
Like an admiring crowd at an execution.

It wasn't the sight of the horses, hounds, and pigeons
Dozing, covered with leaves, in the courtyard,
Or the kitchen fire stopped cold under the spit
Or the flies on the wall, still in a dream-molasses.

And it wasn't the tableau of the maid plucking
A hundred-year-old chicken, or the cook
Caught in the act of tweaking the scullery boy.
He got through those and the cobwebs strung among them

Serene as an heir apparent inspecting corpses.
It wasn't even the King and Queen out cold

On their thrones: the finest dust had smoothed their cheeks,
Had padded the floor, wiped out the tapestries,

And drifted against the unusually polite,
Unnaturally silent ladies-in-waiting
(Prone and supine) and knights as limp as their garters.
But nothing kept him from the winding staircase.

And it wasn't the sight of Sleeping Beauty either.
All her sweet face, though grimy, was meant for kissing.
He puckered, rehearsed in midair, and it seemed easy.
Not even touching cold lips was the hard part.

He touched them. He stood still. He hoped for the best.
(She was the best. Everyone said so.
She was modest and honey-natured, a surefire handful.)
But Sleeping Beauty sat up like Waking Ugly.

She opened one red eye on the Good World,
Bored with it instantly. She had been certain
It had disappeared forever. But here it was: morning,
And time to get up again to be good for nothing.

It had been *exactly* like that from the beginning:
She was too good to be true, a basket case
In a doll basket, pink and gold, as dainty
As a rich dessert with whipped cream and meringue

To be nibbled between meals with smacks of the tongue
And kitchy-coos. But she grew up too true
To be good. Though no one coaxed her to be bad,
Slowly she figured it out, all by herself.

When was life going to happen? Honest to goodness,
Wasn't she honest as the day was long?
But it was *long*. Goodness seemed even longer
Through those long days and evenings till she could dream.

*Day*dreaming didn't do it. She could imagine,
Sure, being humped and crotchety like a witch

Or slick-lipped and languorous like a courtside doxy,
Or cockeyed, creepy, a minimum-lethal-dose

Of a daughter, a whiny changeling whose gold pillow
Belonged *under* the bed where bitches chewed gristle.
But something would always break into those daydreams —
A chuckle under the chin by a cockalorum,

A pinch in the box reserved for royal parties,
Or some Great Oaf like *this* at her bedside.
While she rolled over, snuggling herself to sleep,
He came to the hard part: Getting Out Of There.

He scrambled down the steps, dodged broken-field
Through the throne room where a mixed gaggle of churls
And their grubby, groggy derelict Highnesses
Reared up in rags, all gaping at each other,

Ran past the maid and boy now plucking the cook,
Past flies studding the spitted ham like cloves
Over a fire gone out (with a puff of relief),
Past naked pigeons on clumps of moulted feathers,

Past hounds heel-nipping the horses like hyenas,
And into the gloomiest, thickest part of the thicket
Where a hundred skeletons of his predecessors
(Each, once upon a time, Prince of the Year)

Leaned among brambles, wringing their knucklebones
To welcome him, grinning, covered with roses.

JACK AND THE BEANSTALK

When she saw the bag of beans
He'd brought from the fair — short change
For their old milkless cow —
His mother went as wild
As a giantess in a nightmare.
She called him Fool and Dunce
And bewailed the lost beef-stew,
The cowhide and horn spoons,
Even the glue — all gone,
Thanks to her Simple Simon
Jack and his beanbag
Which she emptied out the window.

As he lay on straw that night,
Hungry, he tried to remember
How the stranger with strange eyes
In a strange reassuring voice
Like a wizard in a dream
Had made him believe in magic,
Had made those beans the strangest
Treasure he'd ever known.
Why had he always believed
In magic, when his elders
Believed only in liars?

He slept, and his heart swelled.
He was growing up. He was swelling
And growing tall as the sky.
In a dream he gathered stars
And flung them across the fields

Of heaven where they sprouted
And bloomed gold in the dawn.

When he woke, the dawn was green
At his window. A vine had grown
Overnight as high as the house,
Had blossomed and turned heavy
With pods, and his mother
Had filled up rows of baskets
With beans to be sold at market,
To be haggled for and eaten.
She had strung the vine and trained it
And now on a tall ladder
Was pruning it with her shears.
"It wants to be a giant,"
She said and went *snip-snap*
To keep those beans near home.

Jack helped like a good boy,
But all day, far overhead,
He heard strange thunder:
It went *Fee-fie-fo-fum*
As if something gigantic
Were stalking around the clouds,
Rumbling and grumbling,
Hunting its bloody supper
And its magic downfall.

THE AUTHOR SAYS GOODBYE
TO HIS HERO

It always seemed obvious what you had to do
Back there at the beginning of the story:
Survive by hacking your way
Past giants and ogresses and clumsy monsters
And witches in the woods toward your true calling
Come lightning, come darkness.
Compared to you, those minor characters
With all their ambushes and bellowing
Seemed incidental tricks,
The harmless, happy accidents due your rank,
Suspenseful nicks in the sword-edges of time.
You left them all
Behind you, forgotten. You were the only one
Going somewhere important, whose life was a wonder
Among wonders, both charmed
And charming against the dullness of those others
Left swollen or headless by the side of the road.
But now, without a chance
To suit yourself to new armor, without warning,
No magic in your words, no light-fingered gifts
Picked up from sorcerers,
And no more suddenly gorgeous messages
Whispered into your ear by gods or demons,
You're on your own.
We're parting company. From this page on,
It's another story, and you won't know quite how
Seriously it may take you:
The very next page you turn may turn out to be
Blank or, worse, may go on twisting and turning
Without your name.

You may even see in a clearing someone striding
Toward you like yourself in a cracked mirror,
A furious fellow-hero
Blundering past your guard and passing behind you.
If so, you may have lost what you thought you'd mastered.
He's on a quest to outdo
All your moon-stricken ventures, his sword even more
Relentlessly carving a trail like the trailblazing
Of blood-red watchfires,
And ahead of you: his abandoned castle, the drawbridge
Down, the feast laid out, brave music,
The throne empty,
And strangers braced for your story's end. No man
Can tell you which will be yours then: princess or crown
Or the glint of the ax.

THE NAVAL TRAINEES LEARN
HOW TO JUMP OVERBOARD

The last trainees are climbing the diving tower
As slowly as they dare, their fingers trembling
On the wet rungs, bare feet reluctantly
Going one step higher, one more, too far
Above the water waiting to take them in.

They stand on top, knees slightly buckled, nowhere
To put their hands, all suddenly thinking how
Good it's always been to be braced up
By something, anything, but ready to be let down
By their loud instructor thirty feet below.

They are the last ones learning how to jump
Feet-first into the swimming pool, to windward
From an imagined ship (in case of drift or fire),

Their ankles crossed, their loose life-jackets held
Down with one hand, their noses pinched with the other.

They pause at the edge. Only one second away
From their unsupported arches, the surface glitters,
Looking too solid, too jagged and broken,
A place strictly for sinking, no place to go.
Each has his last split-second second thoughts.

Others are treading water, hooting and whistling
Abandon Ship and General Alarm,
But these stare toward the emptiest of horizons.
Upright, blue-lipped, no longer breathing, already
Drowned, they commit their bodies to the deep.

ELEGY FOR TWENTY-FOUR SHELVES OF BOOKS

In the restaurant lobby, the owner needed more
Waiting room for people. He redesigned
The bookshelves there (a decorator's notion)
Four inches shallow and sawed off the books.

Now people in that room, waiting for tables,
Can while away their time by browsing titles
Of books with pages shallower by half
And authors' names left cold on half they wrote.

Killing time, some browse the titles for old friends
(*Rescue, The Family Book of Best-Loved Stories*)
Or authors whose works they'd always left till later
To read (*Escape Me Never*), they'd have more time

For stories and lovely books when their families
Grew up and went away (*The World's Great Letters*),

They could escape and never regret the time
Well wasted (*This Rough Magic, Flowering Earth*),

To make the world go away, answer no letters
(*The Pageant of Civilization*), forget TV,
Rough days at work, the waste of the earth (*A Preface
To Critical Reading*), keep off the phone (*The Makers

Of English Fiction*), turn half-forgotten pages
(*Strong Poison, Silent Spring, And Then There Were None*),
Get thinking again, make time for reading, take off
Someplace for a year, use willpower: nothing but books.

But none seem strong enough to spring the glue
Holding books stuck here, tight as their half-owner,
And keeping these Goodwill good-for-nothings in place
(*Adventures in American Literature*).

MARCH FOR A ONE-MAN BAND

He's *a boom a blat* in the uniform
Of an army *tweedledy* band *a toot*
Complete with medals *a honk* cornet
Against *a thump* one side of his lips
And the other stuck with *a sloop a tweet*
A whistle *a crash* on top of *a crash*
A helmet *a crash* a cymbal a drum
At his *bumbledy* knee and a *rimshot* flag
A click he stands at attention *a wheeze*
And plays the Irrational Anthem *bang*.

IN THE BOOKING ROOM

The man with the shopping bag is in so much trouble
He doesn't have nothing to do but have it he's had it
Before God knows and there's nothing to do about it
But set on a bench and wait for the rest of it
To come on down if it wants to and just keep on
Keeping on as usual holding the bag
With fourteen tubes of toothpaste and aftershave
And Brylcreem and Feen-a-mint now why would he want
He never boosted none of that they ask *him*
It was somebody left it there which he had nothing
To do with he must've picked it up like a bundle
You might find laying in the street and there's nothing else
Worthwhile doing but taking a good long look
At the floor and holding a handkerchief dripping blood
Tight over one ear like an empty seashell.

BREATH TEST

He isn't going to stand for it sitting down
As far as he can from the unshaded glare
And the TV camera where he isn't breathing
In no machine no thanks because no way
Being sober as a matter of fact his body
Without a warrant is nobody's damn business
And to a republic for which he isn't
Putting that thing in his mouth as a citizen

Who voted he has a right to disobey
The Law of Supply and Demand by running short
Of supplies and they can all go take a walk
On their own straight line all night if they feel like it.

THE RULES

If you stand still on the sidewalk stand there breathing
With your shoes on not panhandling your pants up
Minding your own damn business only just talking
To yourself to somebody like yourself no mattress
To your name someplace you carry a paper bag
With a bottle in it which you didn't even
Open it yet if you close your eyes for more
Than thirty seconds if you talk too loud
If you're taking a leak singing or dancing
By yourself on god's green earth just sitting just looking
Anyplace too long like the sky like the ocean
Like nothing just figuring which is which or god
Forbid laying down if you're carrying anything
Valuable in the goddamn slightest your own coat
A dozen eggs a bible you stole it come here
You're drunk you're a thief you're drunk get in shut up.

THE ART OF SURRENDER

To be wiped out to the last man would mean missing
All the advantages of giving up.
If you're outmaneuvered and wounded,
Deserted and surrounded,
Act out the painless protocol of surrender:
Your weapons handed over (apparently)
To the apparent victor.
Dignity. Your signature. Heads up, not off.

The winner is also giving up, remember:
No longer struggling with you, no longer winning
But, having prevailed,
Responsible now for all your worldly goods
And (he won't know it yet) your worldly evils.
The full-scale miseries of conquerers
Are yours to deliver
Discreetly with a vengeance from then on.

You must pay the strictest attention, but not attract it,
Must always be one of those far back in the chorus
Droning his praise off-key,
Replastering walls with long-in-the-sweet-tooth slogans
To his greater and grosser glory,
Shaking not spears but those more deadly banners
That will spur him onward
And downward through his hope to outdo the dead.

Then, gentle assassins, help him play the god
And gather near for his command performance.
He will search for love
In your deplorable eyes, but he won't find it

Where he thought it was: at his mercy. Your judgment then
May be more speechless, courtly, and merciless
Than his in a courtyard.
So much for any enemy. He's all yours.

DANSE MACABRE

Come as you are in the dark where the Fiddler's elbow
Is dancing in and out, scratching its music
Bald as a bone across the moonless meadow.

Come quick to the hop of his thumb over the hoarfrost
Into the dying grass and along the stubble
Where the shocked grain of your dreams has gone to harvest.

Come wearing anyone's skin, with a begged or borrowed
Heart in your mouth, footloose, gliding away
From the boredom of that plot, no longer buried,

No longer cast to water or wind as ashes
But feathery, furry, scaly, goodnight-ridden
With all your remnants, all your webby riches.

Between the crescent sun and the dark of the earth,
Come careless under the black flowers in the sky
And the small white stars underfoot, dancing for Death.

CANTICLE FOR XMAS EVE

O holy night as it was in the beginning
Under silent stars for the butchering of sheep
And shepherds, is now and ever shall be, night,

How still we see thee lying under the angels
In twisted wreckage, squealing, each empty eye-slit
Brimful of light as it was in the beginning

Of our slumber through the sirens wailing and keening
Over the stained ax and the shallow grave
That was, is now, and ever shall be, night

Of the night-light, chain and deadlatch by the bolt
Slammed home, the spell of thy deep and dreamless
Everlasting sleep as it was in the beginning

Of the bursting-forth of bright arterial blossoms
From the pastures of our hearts to the dark streets
Shining what is and shall be for this night

Of bludgeons and hopes, of skulls and fears laid open
To the mercies of our fathers burning in heaven,
O little town of bedlam in the beginning
Of the end as it was, as it is to all, good night.

FOUR

YOUR FORTUNE: A COLD READING

When a fortune-teller knows nothing in advance about
a client, he/she is forced to give a "cold reading,"
a fortune applying to almost anyone, but sounding
very personal.

Say nothing revealing. You needn't tell
Anything about yourself or what you suppose
You are or were or what you're going to be.
Give away no secrets. While you sit there, trusting
Nothing you hear, you will hear your fortune.

This is your lucky day, but you don't know
Quite where to turn. Your life is approaching
A sudden climax, but making up your mind
Has always been hard for you. This lack
Of confidence has lost you chance after chance.

Too much of the strongest and most beautiful
Stays hidden in you, unused, neglected:
Your influential ease, your powers of persuasion,
And that gift of inborn charm (through no fault
Of your own) are largely unknown to those around you.

And you deserve far better than that. Now someone
Is coming toward you, older, gray-haired, dark-eyed,
To tell you wonderful news, but you won't listen.
Another person, shorter, pale-eyed, fair-haired,
Is lying to you, and until you know that fact

Your future is shadowed. You stay faithful in love
As long as your love is faithful, but you feel
Dissatisfied, unfulfilled. This nervousness

Is the pivot of your problems. Here at the turning
Point of your life, you must finally choose.

You are more sensitive and romantic now
Than you have ever been. You need love and attention,
But in spite of all you say or do, no matter
What you wear or how you groom your body,
Your heart, your mind, and what you trust is your soul

Feel strangely empty. You have someone only
Halfway into your life, half in strange dreams,
Who will not tell you whether you're close to parting
Or coming closer together. A would-be lover
Is waiting for you, but may soon give up hope.

You gave in once to the conventional world,
Taking its orders, obeying its rules, but lately
Because of your impulsive, heart-led nature,
You have begun to change and have suffered for it
From the tongues of neighbors and friendly hypocrites.

But soon you will learn to trust your own good judgment.
You will live long, be wealthier and wiser.
You don't know how unusual you are.
If you could have the answer to one question
Now, truly, secretly, what would it be?

THE ILLUSIONIST

He had lifted women, helplessly floating,
So many times in his imagination,
He finally gave in to that illusion
And rigged invisible wires and a clever bed
And made it all come true by pretending

(Onstage, to music) to treat his charmed assistant
Lightly, to raise her slowly to midair
Asleep under a sheet like an easy dreamer,
To have her glide his way obediently
And gently, an apparition dead to the world.

But all the while, he knew what the audience
Could only wonder at: her empty form
Under that shroud, sustained by an imitation
Of power in his hands now trembling and powerless
To lift more than themselves at the close of the curtain.

THE OPEN STAIRCASE

(a proposal for a sculpture
in the manner of George Segal)

A staircase without walls,
A dark freestanding
Two-story bare hardwood
Assembly of treads and risers,
Whose zigzagged banisters
Surround a narrow stairwell.

By the newel post at the foot
A stark-white plaster woman
Hesitates, looking up,
Wondering whether climbing
Is better than standing still.
Half down his last few steps,
A white young man is balanced
Off balance, losing his grip.

On the landing, its white torso
As closely curled as a cat's,
Something is sleeping off
The memory of death.
At the brink of the second floor
A girl in her own shut cloud
Of a world hugs her white knees
Against her breast forever.

The man on the upper landing
With hard time on his hands
Stands rigorously nude,
His groin an empty space.

Three steps above, head bent,
A white old man holds on
Before his final flight,
Catching one freezing breath.

At the top, a woman waits.
Her blank face gazes down
Through eyes dissolved in whiteness.
She is expecting no one,
Has nothing behind her back
And nothing to turn to
Or deadlatch after her.
There is no ceiling light.

POEM ABOUT BREATH

(a memory of Elizabeth Bishop, 1950)

She was at work on a poem about breath.
She asked what punctuation might be strongest
For catching her breath, for breath catching
Halfway in her throat, between her straining breastbone
And her tongue, the bubbly catching of asthma.

She didn't care for ellipses or blank spaces.
Would a double colon work? Or Dickinson dashes?
It wouldn't be right for breath to have full stops.
It *does* go on, though people with trouble breathing
Think about it, and breathe, and think about it.

They think too many times of clearing the air
They have to breathe, about the air already
Down there in their lungs, not going out

On time, in time, and when it's finally gone,
Not coming back to the place longing to keep it.

Each breath turns into a problem like a breath
In a poem that won't quite fit, giving the wrong
Emphasis to a feeling or breaking the rhythm
In a clumsy way, where something much more moving
Could happen to keep that poem moving and breathing.

She said as a child she'd learned *one* different style
Of breathing, and her eyelids lowered and darkened.
She bowed her full, firm, pale, remarkable face,
Then solemnly lifted it and opened her mouth,
Stuck out her curled-back tongue and, while it quivered,

Unfolded it slowly, balancing near the end
A half-inch bubble of saliva, gleaming.
With her lightest breath, she puffed it, and it floated
Through late-summer light along the workroom window
All the way to the sill before it broke.

Then she bent over and over, choking with laughter.

STUMP SPEECH

This is the bark, which is always dead.

This is the phloem, which only lives
To carry sunlight down from the leaves,
Then dies into bark, which is always dead.

This is the cambium. Every year
It thickens another ring to wear
And swells the phloem, which only lives

To carry sunlight down from the leaves,
Then dies into bark, which is always dead.

This is the xylem. It lifts the rain
Two hundred feet from root to vein
Out of a cambium well. Each year
It thickens another ring to wear
And swells the phloem, which only lives
To carry sunlight down from the leaves,
Then dies into bark, which is always dead.

This is the heartwood, once locked in
As hard as iron by pitch and resin
Inside the xylem that lifted rain
Two hundred feet from root to vein,
Now soft as cambium out to where
It thickened a final ring to wear,
Then shrank like the phloem that swelled with life
Called down like sunlight from each leaf
Behind the bark, which is always dead.

And this is the stump I stand beside,
Once tall, now short as the day it died
And gray as driftwood, its heartwood eaten
By years of weather, its xylem rotten
And only able to hold the rain
One cold inch (roots withered and gone)
In a shallow basin, a cracked urn
Whose cambium and phloem now learn
To carry nothing down to the dark
Inside the broken shell of the bark
But a dream of a tree forever dead.

And this is the speech that grew instead.

THE WATER LILY

As slowly, as carefully as a wading bird
The elderly Japanese photographer
Comes down stone steps under leaves through pale-green light
To the pond and wavers
At the brink where a single water lily
White around gold lies open. Bending, he stares
Long and, bending farther, moves
Along the bankside, pauses again to gaze,
To focus at last, to shift, to hesitate,
To lift his eyes among wrinkles, to lift one shoulder
And one slow corner of his mouth, to take no picture
But slowly to turn away,
To take nothing away but his mind's eye.

THE FLOWER

A bee fell to the pond, and the light-footed water striders
Came instantly, careless of a wing still blurring the air
(The other a helpless blur under water) and the frantic legs
And the searching extended stinger (no palpable enemy
To shock away or stun into flight) and in half a stunned moment
Had clustered and were at their feast around it, had blossomed
Around the nectar of their gods, all rippling astride a surface
That held them as gently and easily as the reflections
Of sun across maple leaves, and that flower floated and drifted
In silence a withering hour toward the end of summer
Till the petals scattered into the rushes and left nothing.

THE CATERPILLAR

By dense green light
Under a fir bough
It comes down slowly
Through mist over the creek,
As green, as curled
As a willow leaf, not falling
But holding its one strand
Comes down, having fed
All summer, to spin now
The next turn of its way
Down thirty drifting feet
By a thread of itself, being spun
To a beginning, but suddenly
Broken at a touch
Of the headlong current and gone
Downstream and at a splash
And flurry gone again
Into a different dream
In the mouth of a rainbow.

STANDING IN BARR CREEK

Under the down-swept water-wise streaming boughs
Of willows, by boulders whose moss already knows
How to give-in one way without giving up
Anything but the time of day and night,
I stand knee-deep in you to pay my tribute
Of words, one tributary to another.

A piece of paper marked with your name and mine
Declares I'm trying to own eight hundred feet
Of your riparian rights. It's written in water.
It makes no impression on your glittering surface,
Which won't reflect my face, but scatters it
And my blurred shape and mingles them with the sky.

You mill around me casually, steadily
With a relentless calm, in a slow hurry
By your own lights, restlessly, your right of way
A beginning and a simultaneous middle,
A passing-through, an unending dissolution
As permanent as the stones bearing us both.

THREE WAYS OF A RIVER

Sometimes, without a murmur, the river chooses
    The clearest channels, the easy ways
Downstream, dividing at islands equally, smoothly,
And meeting itself once more on the far side
    In a gathering of seamless eddies
That blend so well, no ripples rise to break

Into light like fingerlings taking their first mayflies
    Or, again, it will rush at overhangs
And blunder constantly against bare stone,
Against some huge implacable rock-face
    To steepen and plunge, spring wide, go white,
And be dashed in tatters of spray, revolved and scattered

Like rain clouds pouring forward against a cliff
    In an endless storm of its own making,
While calmly a foot away lies the shape all water
Becomes if it flows aside into a pool,
    As still as the rock that holds it, as level
As if held cold to drink in these two hands.

SNOWFLAKES

*Like most of the sky's snow, which never comes
to earth at all, even the few flakes destined
to reach the ground linger interminably on their
downward journey — in some cases taking weeks or
months on the way . . .*

— Guy Murchie, *Song of the Sky*

They will not fall from high
Above earth, indifferently
Giving in by following
The impulses of others,
But move in their own ways
At a slant through wind after wind

To wobble eccentrically
Edgewise or spin or flutter
Like leaves or go steeply
Feathering down in swirls
Or spirals, each one falling
For days or whole seasons

From the moving peaks of clouds
Where, first by last, they honor
The clear six-crested law
Of their crystal lattices,
And now they are sailing
Softly to drifts at last,

But some, before touching, swerve,
Hover, and rise again,
Their old shapes changing
At first by dwindling, by losing

The small spread branches
They grew from seeds of dust,

Then stretching by gathering
The broken and the lost
Together, each like nothing
Ever before reborn
From the star-filled heart of water,
And stay in the sky forever.

WRITING AN ELEGY IN MY SLEEP

I was mending something between what falls asleep
And what dreams in me. I was closing an emptiness
By threading old words together, by stitching them
Between the night in my mind and the next day.

I knew I was moving certainly toward an end
Already certain. Someone was dead. I wasn't
Mourning but winning a quiet argument
With Death, who had his ear turned to my mouth

As close as Love's ear ever, listening
Calmly to all I cared to say about him
Without a murmur. At the flutter of morning,
I woke and couldn't remember who was missing.

I couldn't remember anything I'd written
On those cream-colored pages evenly
And smoothly and steadily across his silence.
Death is the only one who knows that poem.

WALKING ON THE CEILING

You slip out of bed, your numb feet far away
In the night, and begin to walk on the ceiling
Slowly, taking your time past the chandelier
    Whose crystals have night-bloomed
On a bush, alone at the heart of your new floor,
And step through the doorway over the lintel
(Your threshold now) silently to a passage
    Where the carpet, stretched overhead
Like a lattice for stars, a dimmed-out zodiac,
Glows between you and a floor and a basement
And a foundation masking the face of the earth
    Which has turned to your sky,
An enormous overbearingly heavy heaven
With all the imponderables of firmament
Toward which you lift your eyes, and up the stairwell
    Through the spindly bars
Along the unclimbable overhang of the stairs
You see the clock hung upside down like a bat
And, beyond it, from under the cliff's edge of the eaves,
    Through the window the moonlight
Pouring its pale stream upward. There, you may fall
And be out of your way, away from it all, all night
Till you have nothing between you and the zenith
    But a shadowless daylight.

THE SHAPE

The seed falls, lies still through rain,
Lies covered by snow through its after-ripening,
Then swells in the lengthening days
And bursts, and the primary root
Turns down to make its way
Through the newly dead and the long dead,
And the lateral roots spread wide
To brace for the lifting-up and the opening
Of the caul-pale embryo to the light,
And the roots deepen and darken, and the stem
Hardens and stiffens and lifts higher
The first unfolding leaves and the first branches,
And the roots embrace themselves, embrace stones,
Embrace the earth that holds them, sending their dream
High into the storms of the moon and wind,
The storms of the sun and stars for years.

What falls against the mind and lies still? —
Lies covered and cold, yet ripens,
Spreads down through a wealth of the half-remembered
And the forgotten, the unknown, to a deeper darkness,
To transparent eyes, to the ends of fingers, then raises
Into a storm this branched unreasoning shape?

FIVE:

The Land behind the Wind

1. MAKING CAMP

When their eyes opened, it was more than morning.
They lay by a fallen tree as if it had burned
All night for them, a backlog
Where the true burning came from red crest lichen
And the green blaze of star moss.
There was no other fire except among leaves
Overhead, among leaves beside them.

They had changed. They had been changed. They saw
As clearly as if the air had turned to light
Spineleaf moss and earthstar
Without moving their hands or their bodies,
Map lichen gleaming on rock, not saying where
They were, not saying where to go,
But to begin.

They began making their camp crosswind by water
Facing the southerly bent firebow
Of the sun. They gathered the dead
Branches that had kept the sky from falling
Before falling themselves.
They gathered boughs, a browse bed and a firebed
And, at the turning point, made fire.

2. THEIR FIRE

Their fire was small. They fed it only enough
To keep it through the night and to keep them
Together and unafraid
Lying between it and the face of the cliff
Where, at the foot under a hanging stone,
They had made their shelter
For a time, as others had in years so distant
Now, they seemed as thick and soft as the stillness
Standing around their sleep
In which the animals also slept (the beavers
And otters whose doors were deep under the water,
Squirrels in their hollows)
Or walked in the sleep of others (the gray foxes,
The martens and black bears, silent, listening).
Had they too wondered,
Those other makers of fire, how long to linger
In this same place, how many living seasons
It would keep them warm,
Would hold them together at a single hearthstone
While the round year turned the sky, thickened the clouds
Or thinned them, turning
The snow and the rain as it turned the wind, turned leaves
And turned the color of their hair like ermine's fur
And turned the earth?
They held their hands out to that restless fire
As if to shield it, to calm it, and they turned
Their faces into its light.

3. THEIR SHELTER

They sheltered under a spruce in the sudden storm,
At its foot layered the soft boughs
Of a browse bed and then lay down while rain
And snow mingled along the branches
Above them, around them, in a blue-green darkness.

The tree was their house, its trunk their lodgepole,
A single wall spreading its pungent needles
To waver over their half-sleep, their rooftree
With down-swept rafters whispering
As high as they could hear and far underground.

It spoke all night to them out of the earth,
Out of the sky. It said *the rain,* said *wind,*
Said *snow and ice,* said *deep* and *here.* Their hearts
Were drumming against the night like the wings of grouse.
Their only fire was their hearts against the night.

4. BACKTRACKING

Finding the right way back seemed easy at first:
By glancing aside
At the blazes they'd left only a day ago
(Still bleeding, still white
Even in darkness), they followed their own trail
Through the forest, recalling
Exactly, easily how not to be sidetracked

Where their feet had veered
Before on other paths, at the beckoning
Of the startled and startling
Outcries of birds, moth-flight, the dim retreats
Of wood fern and adder's tongue.
They knew where they were: where they had been before,
Where they had found nothing
To fear, where all they had to do was remember
To take each step
Back by reflecting, and they would find themselves
Again where they'd started.
But gradually by day and gradual evening
The footprints grew fainter.
The leaves had recovered from their careless passage.
The grass had turned
Upright and smooth, no longer bending toward them
In their old direction,
And the bare ground had levelled away their traces
Like snow melting.
They were uncertain whether the marks were theirs
Or from hooves or paws
Or the gouges of fallen branches already gone
Crosspath to earth.
Were those their blazes now or natural scars
Aging and hardening
Over the knots they crowned against hard winter?
How could they know
They were finding their own way back, not someone else's,
Not some stranger's
Who'd been blind-canyoned, who'd blundered out of nowhere
Or into it? There was no way
To tell any longer whether the signs they saw
Underfoot or felt with their fingers
Had been coming or going, whether the ones who'd made them
Were living or dead
Or had turned into the light of a lost clearing
Where everything had begun
And might begin again. They kept on walking,
Dreaming they were there.

5. HIS DREAM

He catches sight of it, finally, in the distance:
The house he had tried so hard to remember
Day after footsore day when, stumbling
Under the burden of sunlight, he had stared
Up canyons, down weathered valleys, only to find
An emptiness once more, a perfectly
Beautiful and beckoning emptiness
Toward which he would stride willingly
And willfully, pacing himself till sundown.

He'd known he would recognize it without knowing
Whether its windows were glass or simply holes,
Whether its roof was slanted and firm — or missing.
He sees someone has lived there, surrounding it
With trees that had once been wild, with wildflowers,
Has smoothed its yard, has cornered and folded down
Grass-beds, has bedded fragments of stone
So feet can find their preordained directions,
Has numbered the lintel, has left the door ajar.

He moves toward it, sleepwalking easily
Over the easy earth, and it lets him in.
What are these rooms? Why are so many walls
Standing unchangeably upright around him?
Why do the floors and ceilings end in corners?
What is there here for him? Nothing remains,
Nothing he wants as deeply as what he's found
Outside of houses, no feeling as full of wonder
As being tired and restless, eager and lost.

And now he dreams he has finished dreaming. His body
Is lying under the pale rooftree of morning,

Under a movable and changeable sky,
And for a moment, only a moment,
He reaches the right true end of travelling,
A place to be still, a place to belong in,
Where forgetting to be himself is the final
Incredible comfort he had always forgotten
Even to wish for. He stands and goes on walking.

6. HER DREAM AND THE AWAKENING

She had become a tree, and two dark birds
Had built their nest in her, had woven
Moss and dead grass
Into a shape no larger than cupped hands
Where now a single egg was gleaming
Like a blackened moon
In the cup of a half-sky, both newly broken
Out of the night. She was in the earth
And above it, and all weather
Was hers alone now. Nothing could fall
That had not already fallen. The birds within her
Sang their first song: silence. Then she saw
Near the ground, making its own small fire,
The woodsman's glistening ax.

She woke in pain. She was lying where she had fallen,
And her mouth was frozen.
Nothing would come from it. Her eyes would not
Open. Had she been thrown down
To this hard ground she could feel
With both her hands? Or had she really chosen
To touch it with so much of her body
At once and yielded her sense of direction
To the long-drawn unrelenting mothering

Call of the earth? The pain was in her heart,
The dungeon at the heart of her rib-caged center
Of balance now telling her it had lost its hold
On her dancing master.
The pain was telling her she was no longer
Held on strings leading up through the dark sky
To those great careless fingers. She heard singing.
Slowly she sat up, and her eyes opened
By themselves. She was in a forest. It was morning.
The woodsman had not killed her. She was flesh
And bone, and the pain was fading
Like all her memories of the terrible palace.
Wild birds and animals had gathered around her,
Looking into her eyes, watching and waiting.

7. THE SOURCE

Neither had said they were going to climb to it,
But they kept walking beside the stream
Under the high shade
Of fir trees, upslope, wading through ferns and leaves
As if through a living and dying current,
Through water itself
Whenever the sea-green walls of the creek bank
Steepened to overhangs where roots
Clung wrong-side up
And seedling firs lurched out from under a world
That dared them to survive one birth.
They shared smooth stones
With sandpipers and dippers, with gold-eyed frogs,
Shared low-slung branches with green herons,
With kingfishers,
Warblers, and winter wrens, who watched them pass
Songless to higher ground, to a light

Thinning out, a waterfall
Where the creek was rain and a sideways mist and past
The sidelong mouths of runnels and freshets
Glistening, as cold
To their fingers' touch as the promises of winter.
More shallow, its stones no longer softened
By white-water crowfoot and pale
Flowerless fountain moss, the creek seemed younger,
Hurrying, its surface quick, more hectic,
As if it felt no longing
Yet to have anything like the sea to turn to.
They climbed past thicker and smaller trees,
Past the half-dead
And the weathered barkless gray dead at the treeline,
Climbed toward spillways of snow on the mountain
Through avalanche lily, sorrel,
Through lupine, through snow, the light a snowfall,
A blue-white daylight the color of snow-melt
Shimmering by their feet,
Still only half persuaded not to be ice
But to give in to the full beginning
Of flowing. At the rim
Of a pond near the foot of steep snow-drifted talus,
Half-frozen, they knelt where the foot-wide creek
Was now being born
Again and again under their eyes. They drank
From the source, their blue lips going numb
At that strange kiss.
They kissed like strangers. They watched the creek spill over
Stones like first words: *Only
Begin, and the rest will follow.*

8. SEEING THE WIND

Long ago, they had tasted a wind like milk. It was still
On their tongues, a claim against earth, and they turned now
In the quiet air and waited for that wind
To come to the horizon. They knew they would know
Its beginning far off, its moving face
Bending the distant grass-heads and tree crowns
Before it, its shape a storm cloud falling forward
To find them. This time, they would welcome it.

They wouldn't find it strange. It had a name
Drawn from its birthplace, not from where it was
At the moment of meeting, not from where it was going
To die. They knew that name, and they saw it
Begin then, coming toward them. They held their eyes
Open to know it, arms open to take it in
Where it belonged, in their bones, not only blowing
Among them as it might through their skeletons

If they lay down, but inside their hollows, a marrow
Like the music of their blood being reborn
Over and over. It came toward their bodies
As they faced into it, becoming what filled them
As the wind became what filled it, what it moved,
And what moved it, and they watched it passing
Through all they knew, through all they had ever known,
Through all they would know tomorrow of love and fear.

9. WALKING INTO THE WIND

After walking into the wind all day, they would rest
Beneath it in the open night, while it murmured
The promises and taunts of a restless lover.
Though they knew where they might shelter, warming their hearts
Among trees and houses, no longer listening
To anything at all in the darkness,
They slept instead where it could touch them
And touch them with its fingers till morning.

They would wake to its whisper then and stand
To face it. Though it veered to a different quarter
Or baffled them, gusting and pausing, dying,
Shifting their landmarks, they would go on walking
Toward it, toward its source. They had known the Country
Of the Blind and the Fortunate Isles by the lovely
Bitter hearsay of elders and lying strangers,
But they dreamed of a place to stand behind the wind.

Before they had faltered to their knees, they found it:
The air fell still, the horizon drew in close,
Binding them in cold arms. Held them turning
Slowly. Encircled them. They turned in circles
As predictably as all lost travellers
Finding no help in any direction, moving
But motionless, holding their bare ground.
There lay the wind at their feet like a pathway.

SIX

LIFESAVING

Those arms stretching toward you helplessly,
Beating the waves and clutching the air,
Want to hang on, they want to hold you close,
Closer forever, not out of love
But fear of losing a way of life by drowning.

No matter how reassuringly you say
To listen and trust you, to relax and give in
To the easy water lifting you together,
That mind staring at you and at nothing
Can't understand *why* it should stop screaming.

One hand is suddenly seizing you, half-strangling,
And one wild crook of an arm is locking
Around your head, and that mind is losing its mind.
Not losing yours, you do what the water
Around you has done already: you give way.

You go away from the light and air, you settle
Downward as if to end the world
Of the head and heart, taking the other with you
As far down as that body will follow
Into the darkness, and it lets you go.

It rises again to the uncertain surface,
No longer thrashing, no longer grappling
Or flailing, out of its wits, but desperately calm.
It believes you now. It's lying still
While your palm is lifting it gently, almost weightless,

The face aimed at the sky, the mind once more
Seeing and listening, remembering

To believe its body can float as well as yours,
That its arms and legs can begin to move
Surely with yours toward the land of the living.

AERIAL ACT

They step into the light,
These two together, free hands held out lightly,
And climb quicksilvered
From the spotlit ring to the ceiling, scattering light
Around them, and begin
There in the crossbeamed intermingling light
To turn in a dance
As their light bodies float almost apart
And return, commingle,
And turn in the air through sure slow plays of light
To stretch, stay one,
And circle again, light-footed, light-handed, light
In a dazzling current,
Adrift in each other's arms, both held and lifted
By streamers of light,
Till they descend once more on glistening strands
To balance lightly
On dust, to stand in a full downpour of light
Surrounded by darkness.

A YOUNG GIRL WITH
A PITCHER FULL OF WATER

She carries it unsteadily, warily
Off balance on bare feet across the room,
Believing wholeheartedly in what she carries
And knowing where she is going carefully
Through the narrow doorway into the sunlight,
Holding by handle and lip what she begins
To pour so seriously and slowly now, she leans
That way as if to pour herself. She grows
More and more light. She lightens. She sees it flowing
Away from her to fill her earth to the brim.
Then she stands still, smiling above flowers.

A WOMAN STANDING IN THE SURF

Thigh-deep in the sea, she watches waves arriving
As if those storms
Thousands of miles away in starry spirals
Or the long upheavals
Of fire from the ocean bed or the almost breathless
Breathless baffling
Of winds by the moon had all been brought to bear
And to light on this shore
For her alone, each having known all along
Where she was waiting
And how to touch her coldly, billowing gently

Or suddenly surging
As she rises to meet them, crying out out of fear
Of her desire, in wonder
Outspreading her arms over water to welcome them
Against her, against her.

A YOUNG WOMAN FOUND IN THE WOODS

Lying among flowers in a green shadow,
She has left the cage that held her breath and her heart
To the wind, a hovel where rain, not blood, is flowing
Breathlessly, heartlessly.

Though her brow has cleared, her eyes have grown more hollow
Than when they wondered where on earth they were,
Turned inward now to a private emptiness
With no horizon.

Her tongue and lips have taken separate ways
To leave her speechless. She is smiling at strangers
More openly than ever at any lover
And has no secrets.

A WOMAN FEEDING GULLS

They cry out at the sight of her and come flying
Over the tidal flats from miles away,
Sideslipping and wheeling
In sloping gray-and-white interwoven spirals
Whose center is her
And the daily bread she casts downwind on the water
While rising to spread her arms
Like wings for the calling of still more gulls around her,
Their cries intermingling at the end of daylight
With the sudden abundance
Of this bread returning after the hungry night
And the famine of morning
And the endlessly hungry opening and closing
Of wings and arms and shore and the turning sky.

WAKING UP IN A GARDEN

We wake together, discovering the garden
Has gone to sleep around us, the sky dead black.
We've nearly forgotten
The when and where of love that brought us here
And left us near sundown, the why and how of our lives
At the familiar strange beginning of night.

The moths are hovering at the shadows of flowers,
Engrossed by their blurred labors, some zigzagging

Wildly, cross-purposefully,
And some in whorls like nebulae, constellations
Unstrung from the belt of their small zodiac
To fade and waver down into the grass.

And sweeping by, the bats are taking others
Silently and carefully into silence.
A nighthawk, the back-swept
Outlines of its wings dark crescent moons,
Swoops near again and again. The moths vanish,
Reappear and vanish, die, spin back transformed,

And we lie under this feast like part of it,
Not wishing ourselves the sure wings of the hunters
But, lighter than feathers,
The baffling erratic uncontrollably crooked
Night-bearing gifted star-marked wings of the hunted
Whose tongues, like ours, go spiralling into sweetness.

BITTER CHERRY
————————

The pruner, his saw ready,
Said there was no room
For that weed in the garden,
It should go down and out,
And shook his head, looking sour
When I said I wanted to spare
The wild bitter cherry
Where a bird had dropped a seed
One autumn and planted it
Like a birth-tree in a year
When nothing else was born.

Nothing else could have made
Its way up through

The tangled barricades
Of holly in that cramped corner
Or struggled toward a light
Already taken and held
Against all comers,
But slowly wedging thin branches
Past the chevaux-de-frise
And thorny scarps where even
The quick quickset kinglets
And wrens had found slow going,
At last it straightened
And broadened above the fence,
Above its fruitless cousins
(Grafted for show and tamed
From greenhouse to nursery),
And it bloomed in a glimmering
Of sparse, hard-pitted stars
That ripened and reddened
And darkened a bitter crop,
And the robins and waxwings
Have come this September day
All day in its honor.

REPLANTING A GARDEN

Here, roses sickened in the shade of a house
Where only north light or the last light of evening
Could reach them. They would grope for a season,
Then moulder and thin out, as flowerless
As moss and quillwort covering their roots
Or fungus caring for their slow deaths like nurslings.

So day by dawn, by storm or half-clouded sky,
He made his way through the woods

Where the dense crowns of fir and hemlock closed
A shade still deeper than house-shade, where sun
And rain fell, not as themselves, but as each other
(Light showers of light, light rain) to the forest floor.

And he knelt there to sword fern and deer fern,
Oak fern and holly fern, unearthing them gently
And wrapping their cool rootstocks for transplanting.
From the lips of pools, from creek banks and spring banks
And the feet of watersheds (their supple black-stemmed
Aureoles wavering) he brought maidenhair

And took whole sides of crumbling stumps in his arms,
Each bearing clusters of wood fern and shield fern,
And brought them home and laid them down in the garden
And stood beside their deepening, changing forms,
One earthbound frond at a time all summer long
Uncoiling life after life out of that shadow.

THE GARDENER'S DREAM

By moonlight he saw roses already climbing
Over the wall and into the wild fields
Where they budded and bloomed even as he was gazing
From the middle of the garden: foxgloves and columbine
Were lifting their stalks to blossom beyond his gateway
Downhill to a stream bed and across it into a forest
Among cryptantha, purslane, and bleeding heart.
Their seeds as they touched the earth were swelling and bursting
At once and rooting, unfolding, springing upward
Across a whole valley. The borders he'd planted and culled
As seedlings had sprawled out of order, their careful rows,
Their circles and squares and oblongs
Had gone astray and were stretching at random

Across his paths, their colors brightening
With stems and calyces brought back from the dead,
And almost at hand, pale flower-heads turned to him
In the morning as if expecting light and rain
To spill from his fingers.

EARTHBIRD

It flies through sand and shale under the ground
Among stones, through stone,
Through quartz and gold, down granite, through black rivers
(Its underworldly wind),
Through bones and shells dust-bedded in dry seas,
Through crystal, through clay
And pumice, under the spurs of mountains, through frozen
Muskeg and tundra, its claws
Obsidian-sharp, slant-winged, its feathers glinting,
Its beak piercing
All lost weathers under the faces of earth,
Its cries almost silent
Like pebbles scattering, now rising, whispering
Through the hanging gardens
Of roots where earthbird perches and stares upward
At the land suspended
Over its head like clouds, at our fires burning
Down through its night
More dimly than moons and stars, where it knows them,
Where it waits for our return.

MOSS CAMPION AT THE SNOW LINE

The last wildflower before
The beginning of everlasting
Snow has bloomed bright rose
At the edge of whiteness
From under the no longer
Melting drifts at the end
Of summer. Its narrow leaves
Have tightened, have closed around
Each other in a mass
Stiff-green as stones. Its taproot
Far back inside a crevice
Holds all the way into ice.
It has been here
Before, has survived as its own
Long-dying ancestor
On the verge beside the last
Of light-fall. Lying still
Beside a winter as constant
As this mountain, it will go
Under once more to endure
After the first snow
One more burial.

SONG AFTER MIDNIGHT

Where have you been, Two-legged Walker?
To marsh, to thicket, to the bones of trees.
And what have you brought from there
For your Strange Sister?
Dry leaves like hands and the dumb-show of rain.
Go back again.
Find her the flower whose roots stretch up through the air
And bloom all winter.

Where else have you gone, Climber on All Fours?
To gardens of stones, to the feet of mountains.
And what have you brought from there
For your Strange Mother?
Thornapple, mallow, wingscale, vetchling, felwort.
Go back once more.
Find her the eyeteeth of Eagle, feathers of Marmot,
Claws of Blue Racer.

What other paths have you stumbled on, Listener?
The riverside, the river's mouth, and the seashore.
And what have you brought from there
For your Strange Lover?
The spinning of countless crescent moons in the water.
Go back to that dancing.
Find her the turn of her salt-breathing blood
In the heart of weather.

And where will you go next, Quick-and-Dead Tale-teller?
To a house, to a room, to an old darkness.
And what will you bring from there

For the Witch of Dreamers?
Starleaf, stoneroot, earthtide, the kiss of the spider.
Lie down alone
Till you can ask one true beautiful question
Without an answer.

SEVEN

THE SONG

At first, he sang for love
Of singing and for one
Who laughed and wept and listened.

He sang to water falling
On sand and the steep woods
And streaming against stone.

He sang in the cold
For the lives and deaths of birds
And forests and elders.

And then he sang to be
Believed, waiting alone
Under a shut window.

On the shore, at the feet of trees,
By a creek, by a silent house,
He changed to what he sang

And became for a time nothing
But a voice in the distance
Touching the ears of others.

And now he sings again
For love in a way no stranger
Or lover will ever hear

Without remembering her
In his arms, no matter where
Or how that singing ends.

THAT MOMENT

Having swum farther than he'd known he could swim, so far
He'd stopped looking for land
And had simply gone on swimming and swimming till his arms
Slowed, exhausted,
And his legs, no longer fluttering, faltering out of time
With his heart, began
To settle slowly deeper and deeper into water
(For all he knew
Deeper than any water he'd ever crossed), that moment
His feet, instead of nothing, touch
The soft upflow of earth to bear them, and he starts breathing
Almost as if each breath
Might follow another, as if he could depend on knowing
From this breath forward
That his body, though nearly weightless, might move once more
Light-stepped, as buoyant
As light on the face of the moon, alive after all
That dying, that moment
He turns and walks toward her in a room, his love
For her that moment beginning.

SLEEPING ALONE

It should be easy: no one breathing
Beside him, no one restlessly turning
Toward or away from him in the darkness,

No fingers in sleep by chance meeting
That other body, and no whimpering
Through the shut door of a nightmare
(Except from his own), even oblivion
All his this night if he could only
Find it and keep it, but waking alone
To watch the divided stage of his mind
Going dim by turns and lights rising
One slow side at a time on her sleeping
Far too far from him with no one
Beside her but an emptiness
Like his, like the emptiness he turns to
Hourly emptily without her.

A GUIDE TO THE FIELD

Through this wild pasture, this mile of strewn grasses,
We walk among seed crowns
Only half-formed at the beginning of summer
But already growing
Heavier with the burdens nothing will harvest
But birds and the weather,
Some (this ryegrass) like caterpillars spinning
Cocoons out of sunlight,
And some (this lavender bluegrass) a waist-high forest
Of slender fir trees,
Still others (cheatgrass, wild barley) plotted like flowerbeds
Under flights and counter-flights
Of swallows and field sparrows. Each blade, each spikelet,
Each glume and awn, each slowly
Stiffening stem, no matter what may come
In the next wind — hail or fire —
Will take its beheading, will give up this year's ghost
With less than a murmur,

And we pass beside them now, taking together
Our first strange steps
On a path that leads us down to its end in water.
Each look, the first.
Each touch of our strange fingers, the first again.
Each movement of our bodies
As strangely startling as what the swallows dare
Skimming the pond, their wingtips
Glancing, glancing again, swept-luminous crescents,
Each act of theirs
As if for us only. They show us ways to turn
Into willing lovers
Not needing to say *Yes* on this day when all questions,
Even before the asking,
Have mingled with their answers. Remember winter:
Birds gone, seeming lost,
And the grass lying down once more to pretend one death,
Dried pale and brittle
By a hard-earned hard-learned gift of seeming done
With its life. Love dies, and love
Is born at the same heart-roots in words once cold
And comfortless as a scattering
Of ashes: *All flesh is grass* meaning *Love lies down
Mortal, immortal.*

GETTING AWAY

We had brought our love there: to a lake by a forest
And by nightfall at the firelit hearthstone lay
Together to whisper it, to become it,
To dream it. But something wanted out of the closet.

The rat-scratching began at the inner threshold,
Moved up the jamb and scratched at the lintel

And went scuffling left and right along bare walls,
Searching a way out but falling and scrabbling.

We had met life from the woods already, gray-and-white
Mouse-heads peeking tremulously between floorboards,
And had heard them tip-tailing carefully from spring
To spring in the loveseat, holding their nesting ground,

And in their behalf, and in love's, had decided to live
And let live, to share the bread we'd broken
Under this roof where they were as safe from claws
As we were from new preachments and old orders.

But this was no subtle mousy deferential
Skittering. It was an unabashed declaration
Of independence by something as good as lovers
At making and having its way and getting away.

We tried pounding the door, imagining wood rats
Like city rats would have the self-regard
To quit and go into hiding and come back later
When they would have themselves to themselves like us.

But the scratches went on, not pausing, went on
And on without fear, without flinching, without shifting
To the ceiling or underfoot on whatever passage
This fellow creature had gnawed and wriggled through.

So at last with brooms and boots and the righteous courage
Of tenancy (our self-possession being
Nine points of our law) we braced ourselves
To face the tenth, having propped the porch door wide

To tempt it into the hospitality
Of the night where it would be welcome naturally
And opened the closet door, while cringing sideways,
And saw the tawny-backed slender snow-breasted weasel

Standing erect, the small paws dangling, gazing
From brooms to us more calmly than possible

And tilting a small incredibly sinuous head
And neck on its shoulderless body, slowly deciding

To let us go on being where we were
Whatever we were, whatever we meant to be,
And it bent at the baseboard and glided on all fours
Around the corner and out the door down the stairs

More smoothly and silently than the evening
Had climbed them, and disappeared into the darkness
And left us and the mice in that good house
Where nothing stirred but all of us till morning.

IN LOVE

Before arriving at love, our only problems
Were what to do all day
And all night. Good works? Remembering our makers?
Perpetual prayer
At the grinding wheels of fortune or taking turns
Like the earth beneath us
From shadow to shadow? The passionate reenactment
Of pasts whose grievances
Seemed near and too dear, as sour as a miser's dream
Of gold from nowhere?
Or counting our sad blessings backwards to zero?
But now we sleep
And wake in the wildly abandoned countrysides
Of our bodies, embodying
Whole days and nights while Time keeps time, keeps time
With our preoccupied hearts.

FOR A WOMAN SITTING BY A CREEK

At your side, I watch you stare
At a stream rushing away
And see your eyes become
That glittering traveller,
Never still yet holding
A stillness in a blur
Down to its stones (the colors
Of everything earthly)
Where shafts of sunlight
Have ended their steep journey
On a creekbed below the cold
Incessantly altering
Downheaval of current.

That stream stays what it is
All day, all night, through winters
When no one waits beside it.
Though it may change like you
Quick moment by still moment
Under a sun once more
Sinking beyond us, your eyes,
Love, drinking their fill,
Are holding through the swirl
And spill of eddies whatever
May glint in passing, moved
And held, being all water
May do or turn to,
Translucent, gathering light.

OUR BLINDNESS

I see you now, and now
With the sudden end of lamplight
At the bedside have lost you
For a brief while to the night
Except for the pale drift
Of the pillow beside your face
And, over your landscape,
The softly touching whiteness
Of the sheet like a bed of snow.

Now love is blind. We move
To find what we can't see
Across the strange familiar
Neighborhood of our bodies
Like the blind when a snowfall
Has muffled and smoothed away
All shapes from their feet and fingers
To make a second blindness.
We turn to all we know.

BY STARLIGHT

Now far from those harsh lights and the glare over cities, alone
By a clearing in a forest, we lie down
For the first time in our lives
Together under stars

And, keeping the earth in its place behind our backs, we stare
Upward into the ancient stream of starlight
Whose current, though it appears
To falter, to waver,
Has made its way to our eyes through barely imaginable
Down-curved ravines of space to dazzle us
With its streamers and wildfires,
Its ice-laden glitter,
The unconstellated burning rubble of godlings, outcast
And spilled from the zodiac and constantly falling
As they have always fallen
Even before eyes turned
To wonder and will go on falling whether we stay to watch
Or soon give back our small share of the spectrum
To the oldest of nights, to the expansive
Gestures of a universe
We share so pointedly: some (see there) bloomed long ago
And dimmed, yet shine through lifetimes without a source,
With no beginning left
Behind them now
To begin with, but only an ever-shortening reach of glory
That flickers in darkness. All will consume themselves
And be reborn, as we are
Here, having followed
Their example, love, as fixed and erring and fair and steadfast,
Not star-crossed yet, but truly catching them
As they slant to us past hemlocks, as rich
And clear as our silence.

FIRST LIGHT

Before first light no sound
From the woods or the calm lake
Steel-gray in mist to its end
And even the creek's down-rush
On a stone bed gone still
As the owl that spoke for us
All night out of the hemlocks.

But now from the forest floor
(Dark green in a slow rain)
The voice of the winter wren —
Just as a touch of sun
Enlightens this good morning —
Begins its long cascading
Spillways and white rapids.

I see you wake, not moving
More than your eyelids
To listen, still half-held
By your dream, which was also mine
Between the owl and the wren:
That we'd learned how to fly
And sing by dark, by daylight.

You see my eyes have opened
With yours. Each of us turns
To the other, arms outstretched,
Then closed, both newly fledged
But as wing-sure at wakening
As owl-flight or wren-flight
And as song-struck as this dawn.

ACKNOWLEDGMENTS

AMERICAN POETRY REVIEW: *Waking Up in a Garden*

AMICUS JOURNAL: *A Remarkable Exhibition; For a Fisherman Who Dynamited a Cormorant Rookery; Winter Wren*

ANTAEUS: *The Land behind the Wind*

ANTIOCH REVIEW: *Snowflakes*

THE ATLANTIC: *The Author of* American Ornithology *Sketches a Bird, Now Extinct; Washing a Young Rhinoceros; Stump Speech; A Young Woman Found in the Woods*

BENNINGTON REVIEW: *Octopus; Sleeping Beauty; The Naval Trainees Learn How to Jump Overboard; Elegy for Twenty-four Shelves of Books*

CORNFIELD REVIEW: *In the Plaza de Toros*

GEORGIA REVIEW: *The Art of Surrender; Canticle for Xmas Eve*

INDIANA REVIEW: *That Moment*

IOWA REVIEW: *Feeding; Kingfisher; The Shape*

KANSAS QUARTERLY: *The Author Says Goodbye to His Hero*

KAYAK: *The Best Slow Dancer; Your Fortune: A Cold Reading*

KENYON REVIEW: *A Woman Standing in the Surf*

MALAHAT REVIEW: *A Young Girl with a Pitcher Full of Water*

MEMPHIS STATE REVIEW: *Elephant Ride; Danse Macabre*

MID-AMERICAN REVIEW: *Standing in Barr Creek; Three Ways of a River*

MISSOURI REVIEW: *The Open Staircase*

THE NATION: *Pandora's Dream; The Illusionist; The Caterpillar; A Woman Feeding Gulls; Bitter Cherry*

THE NEW REPUBLIC: *My Father in the Basement; In the Booking Room; Breath Test*

THE NEW YORKER: *Golden Retriever; Getting Away*

OHIO JOURNAL: *The Storyteller*

POETRY: *Their Bodies; To a Farmer Who Hung Five Hawks on His Barbed Wire; The Horsemen; Under the Raven's Nest; March for*